The Funniest Houston Texans Joke Book Ever

Copyright

Version 1

Unofficial and unauthorized

This book is a joke book, written in a light hearted way.

No offence is meant to any person or group of people

Read, laugh and enjoy a joke

Introduction

Thank you for taking the time to read "The Funniest Houston Texans Joke Book Ever". In this book we take a light hearted look at football and our rivals.

We have scoured the country for some of the best and funniest jokes, most jokes were thought up at the stadium or in the bar after a game and a few beers.

This book covers some of the best jokes; no joke has been kept

out of this book for being
politically incorrect or too rude.

Get ready to share a laugh at our
rival's expense ...

St. Peter was manning the Pearly Gates when 40 Titans fans showed up. Never having seen a Titans fan at heaven's door, St. Peter said he would have to check with God. After hearing the news, God instructed him to admit the 10 most virtuous from the group.

A few minutes later, Saint Peter returned to God breathless and said, "They're gone."
"What? All of the Titans fans are gone?" asked God.

"No" replied Saint Peter "The Pearly Gates!"

What is the difference between a Titans fan and a coconut? One's thick and hairy and the others a tropical fruit

Three old football fans are in a church, praying for their teams.

The first one asks, "Oh lord, when will we get to the Super Bowl?" God replies "In two years' time"
"But I will be dead by then", said the old man.

The second fan asks "When will we next win the Super Bowl?"
"In ten years' time", God replies
But I'll be dead by then, said the old man

The last man asks "When will the Titans win the Super Bowl?" God thinks and then says "I will be dead by then"

Rumour has it that to cut the cost of the repairs to the Titans scoreboard, only the light bulbs in the half used to show the opponents score will be fixed.

The other half will just have 'Titans 0' painted on in yellow paint.

The Titans are apparently under investigation by the IRS for tax evasion; they've been claiming for Silver Polish for the past 10 years.

What's the difference between a female Colts fan and a pit bull?

Lipstick

There was once a fanatical Texans fan who thought of nothing but football all day long. He talked about football, read about football, watched nothing but football on television and attended games as often as he possibly could.

Finally his poor wife could not stand it any longer. One night she said, 'I honestly believe you love the Texans more than you love me!'

'Gosh,' said the fan, 'I love the Steelers more than I love you!'

I've started watching the Colts, as my doctor says I should avoid any excitement.

Top tip for Colts fans: don't waste money on expensive new jerseys every season.

Simply strap a large inflatable penis to your forehead, and everyone will immediately know which team you support.

One of the highest paid players in the NFL, John had everything going for him. He had an expensive new mansion, a new sports car, a wardrobe full of designer clothes.

His only problem was that he had three girlfriends and he couldn't decide which one to marry. So he decided to give $5,000 to each woman to see what she would do with it.

The first woman bought new clothes for herself and had an expensive new hairdo, a massage, facial, manicure and pedicure.

The second woman bought a top-of-the range DVD and CD player, as well as an expensive set of golf clubs and tennis racquet and gave them all to John. "I used the money to buy you these gifts because I love you," she told him.

The third woman invested the money in the stock market, and within a short time had doubled her investment. She gave John back the initial $5,000 and reinvested the profit. "I'm investing in our future because I love you so much," she said.

John considered carefully how each woman had spent the money, and then married the woman with the biggest breasts.

A quarterback had a particularly bad season and announced that he was retiring from professional football. In a television interview he was asked his reasons for quitting the game.

'Well, basically,' he said, 'it's a question of illness and fatigue.'

'Can you be more specific?' asked the interviewer.

'Well,' said the player, 'specifically the fans are sick and tired of me.

A woman goes to see the doctor.

"Doctor, doctor, I'm very worried about my son," she said. "All he does is play football all day; then he comes in covered in mud and walks all over my clean carpet."

"I think you may be over-reacting," said the doctor reassuringly. "Sons often behave like that"

"I know, doctor," said the woman, "but it's not just me that's worried about him. His wife is too"

My wife told me last week that she'd leave me if I didn't stop spending so much time at football games.

'What a shame!'

'Yes. I shall miss her'

A woman was reading a newspaper one morning and said to her husband,

'Look at this, dear. There's an article here about a man who traded his wife for a season ticket to the Texans. You wouldn't do a thing like that, would you?'

'Of course I wouldn't!' replied her husband. 'The season's almost over!'

Snow White arrived home one evening to find her home destroyed by fire. She was especially worried because she'd left all seven dwarves asleep inside. As she scrambled among the wreckage, frantically calling their names, suddenly she heard the cry: "The Titans for the Super Bowl."

"Thank goodness," sobbed Snow White. "At least Dopey's still alive!"

The ASPCA have acted swiftly after recent results.

If you see any Titans fans walking a dog please call them immediately on 6-0, 6-6, 6-12, 6-18, 6-24 as they're not very good at holding on to leads

Four surgeons are taking a coffee break:

1st surgeon says "Accountants are the best to operate on because when you open them up, everything inside is numbered"

2nd surgeon says "Nope, librarians are the best. Everything inside them is in alphabetical order"

3rd surgeon says "Well you should try electricians. Everything inside them is color coded"

4th surgeon says "I prefer Titans fans. They're heartless, spineless, gutless and their heads and butts are interchangeable"

How do you change a Titans fans mind?

Blow in his ear!

What's the difference between a Titans fan and a broken clock?

Even a broken clock is right twice a day

What's the difference between a Titans fan and a coconut?

You can get a drink out of a coconut

Two guys were walking through a cemetery when they see a tombstone that read: "Here lies John Smith, a good man and a Colts fan"

So, one of them asked the other: "When the hell did they start putting two people in one grave?"

Two Titans fans jump off a cliff.
Which one hits the ground first?

Who gives a F**k!

What do you get when you cross a Titans fan with a pig?

I don't know, there are some things a pig just won't do

What do you call a Cowboy fan on the moon?

A Problem

What do you call 100 Cowboy fans on the moon?

An even bigger problem

What do you call all the Dallas Cowboys fans on the moon?

Problem solved

How do you define 199 Colts fans

Gross Stupidity

Why did the Colts go on the stock market?

To prove that crap can float

Why do Colts fans whistle
whilst sitting on the john?

So they know which end to wipe

What's the difference between a Titans fan and an Onion?

No one cries when you chop up a Titans fan!

Did you hear that the postal service just recalled their latest stamps?

They had photos of Cowboys players on them, people couldn't figure out which side to spit on

How many Titans fans does it take to pave a driveway?

Depends how thin you slice them

What would you call a pregnant Titans fan?

A dope carrier

What do you call a Titans fan with half a brain?

Gifted

What do Titans fans use as birth control?

Their personalities

How many Colts supporters does it take to stop a moving Bus?

Never enough

What do you call a Titans fan with no arms and legs?

Trustworthy

What's the difference between a dead dog in the road and a dead Colts fan?

Skid marks in front of the dog

What's the difference between a Titans fan and a Vibrator?

A Titans fan is a real dick

If you see a Colts fan on a bicycle, why should you never swerve and hit him?

You don't want to damage your bike

What would you call two Colts fans going over a cliff in an SUV?

A complete waste of space. You could have squeezed six of them into one of those

What's the difference between a
Titans fan and a bucket of crap?

The bucket

How do you get a one armed Titans fan down from a tree?

Wave at him

How do you keep a Titans fan busy?

Put him in a round room and tell him to sit in the corner

What do Colts fans and mushrooms have in common?

They both sit in the dark and feed on nothing but crap

How many Colts fans does it take to change a light bulb?

It doesn't matter, because they're all condemned to eternal darkness

Mike Munchak was going to the Titans Halloween party dressed as a pumpkin

But at midnight he still hadn't turned into a coach

How is a pint of milk different than a Colts fan?

If you leave the milk out for a week it develops a culture

What's the difference between a Colts fan and a sperm?

At least a sperm has one chance in 5 million of becoming a human being

There's a rumor going about that if you buy a season ticket at LP Field then you get a free space suit.

Apparently it's due to the lack of atmosphere

How do you save a Titans fan from drowning?

Take your foot off his head

What's the difference between a
busload of Titans fans and a
Hedgehog?

On a hedgehog, the pricks are
on the outside

What do Hemorrhoids and Titans fans have in common?

They're both a complete pain in the ass and never seem to go away completely

Why did the Colts fan climb the glass window?

To see what was on the other side

What's the difference between a Colts fan and a Chimp?

One's hairy, stupid and smells, and the other is a chimpanzee

An anxious woman goes to her doctor. "Doctor," she asks nervously, "I'm a bit worried - can you get pregnant from anal intercourse?"

"Of course," replies the doctor, "Where do you think Titans fans come from?"

How do you kill a Titans fan when he's been drinking?

Slam the toilet seat on his head

What's the difference between Pamela Anderson and the Titans line?

Pam's only got two tits in front of her

Santa Claus, the tooth fairy, an intelligent Colts supporter and an old bum are walking down the street together when simultaneously they each spot a fifty dollar bill. Who gets it?

The old bum, of course - the other three are mythical creatures

How can you tell a level headed Titans fan?

He dribbles from both sides of his mouth - at the same time

Newsflash

Thieves broke into the home of a Colts fan and stole two books. "The thing that upsets me", he said "is that I hadn't finished coloring them in yet!"

What do you get if you cross a Monkey with a Titans fan?

Nothing. Monkeys are far too clever to screw a Titans fan

What is the difference between a
battery and a Titans fan?

A battery has a positive side

What's the difference between the Titans defense and a taxi driver?

A taxi driver will only let in four at a time

What do Colts fans and laxatives have in common?

They both irritate the crap out of you

What's the ideal weight for a Titans fan?

Three pounds, that's including the Urn

Two Titans fans are on the plane on the way to a game

One turns to the other and says "Hey John! If this plane turns upside-down will we fall out?"

"No way Steve," says his friend "of course we'll still be pals!"

You're trapped in a room with a Lion, a snake and a Titans fan. You have a gun with two bullets. What should you do?

Shoot the Titans fan, twice

What do you call a Cowboys fan in a suit?

The accused

Why did God make Colts fans smelly?

So blind people could laugh at them too

What do you call 100 Colts fans
at the bottom of a cliff?

A good start

What do you call a dead Titans fan in a closet?

Last year's winner of the hide and seek contest

What do you call a Titans fan that does well on an IQ test?

A cheat

What has 100,000 arms and an IQ of 170

LP Field during every game

Why do people take an instant dislike to Colts fans?

It saves time

What do you say to a Colts fan with a job?

Can I have a Big Mac please

What do you get if you see a Titans fan buried up to his neck in sand?

More sand

What's the difference between a Colts fan and a shopping cart?

The cart has a mind of its own

A Cowboys fan goes to his doctor to find out what's wrong with him.

"Your problem is you're fat" says the doctor

"I'd like a second opinion" responds the man

"OK, you're ugly too" replies the doctor

A Texans and Colts fan get into a nasty car accident. Both vehicles are really wrecked, but amazingly neither of them are hurt.

After they crawl out of their cars, the Texans fan says, "So you're a Colts fan, that's interesting. I'm a Texans fan.

Wow! Just look at our cars. There's nothing left, but fortunately we are unhurt. This must be a sign from God that we should meet and be friends and live together in peace the rest of our days."

The Colts fan replied, "I totally agree, this must be a sign from God!"

The Texans fan went on, "And look at this - here's another miracle. My car is completely demolished but this bottle of Jack Daniels didn't break. Surely God wants us to drink it, to celebrate the fact we are alive?"

He hands the bottle to the Colts fan, who nods his head in agreement, opens it and takes few big swigs from the bottle, then hands it back to the Texans fan.

The Texans fan takes the bottle, immediately puts the cap back on, and hands it back to the Colts fan. The Colts fan asks, "Aren't you having any?"

The Texans fan replies, "Nah ... I think I'll just wait for the cops"

A truck driver used to keep himself amused by scaring every Cowboys fan he saw walking down the Street in their jersey. He would swerve as if to hit them, and at the last minute, swerve back onto the road.

One day as he was driving along the road, he saw a priest hitch-hiking. He thought he would do his good deed for the day and offer the priest a lift.

"Where are you going, Father?" he asked.

"I'm going to say mass"

"No problem," said the driver, "Jump in and I'll give you a ride"

The priest climbed into the truck and they set off down the road. Suddenly the driver sees a Cowboys fan on the sidewalk, and instinctively swerved as if to hit him, but just in time, remembering the priest in his truck, swerved back to the road again, narrowly missing the idiot.

Although he was certain that he didn't hit him, he still heard a loud "Thud". Not understanding where the noise came from, he glanced in his mirrors, and, seeing nothing, said to the priest, "Oh sorry Father, I nearly hit that Cowboys fan"

"No need to apologize Son," replied Father, "I got the ba*tard with the door!"

What's the difference between OJ Simpson and the Colts?

OJ at least had a defense

What do they call a drug ring in Dallas?

A huddle

What's the difference between the Tennessee Titans and Cheerios?

Cheerios belong in a bowl

Wanna hear a joke?

The Tennessee Titans

What's the difference between a vacuum cleaner and the Titans?

There's only one dirt bag in a vacuum cleaner

What did the Titans fan say after his team won the Super Bowl?

"Dammit mom, why'd you wake me up? I was having an amazing dream!"

How are the Colts like my neighbors?

They can't pick up a single yard

Want to hear a Titans joke?

Matt Hasselbeck

Why is Matt Hasselbeck like a grizzly bear?

Every fall he goes into hibernation

What's the difference between the Colts and a dollar bill?

You can still get four quarters out of a dollar bill

What do the Colts and possums have in common?

Both play dead at home and get killed on the road

What is the difference between a
Titans fan and a baby?

The baby will stop whining after
a while

How many Colts players does it take to change a tire?

One, unless it's a blowout, in which case they all show up

What do you call 53 millionaires around a TV watching the Super Bowl?

The Dallas Cowboys

What do the Colts and Billy Graham have in common?

They both can make 70,000 people stand up and yell "Jesus Christ"

How do you keep a Colts player out of your yard?

Put up goal posts

Why are so many Titans players claiming they have the Swine Flu?

So they don't have to touch the pigskin

How do you stop a Titans fan from beating his wife?

Dress her in a Texans jersey

If you have a car containing a Cowboys wide receiver, a Cowboys linebacker, and a Cowboys defensive back, who is driving the car?

The cop

How do you castrate a Colts fan?

Kick his sister in the mouth

What should you do if you find three Dallas Cowboys fans buried up to their neck in cement?

Get more cement

What's the difference between a Titans fan and a carp?

One is a bottom-feeding, scum sucker, and the other is a fish

How did the Titans fan die from drinking milk?

The cow fell on him

What does a Colts fan do when his team wins the Super Bowl?

He turns off the PlayStation

What do you call a Dallas Cowboy in the Super Bowl?

A referee

Did you hear that the Titans football team doesn't have a website?

They can't string three "W's" together

What does a Titans fan and a bottle of beer have in common?

They're both empty from the neck up

Why do Colts fans keep their season tickets on their dashboards?

So they can park in handicap spaces

How do you keep a Titans fan from masturbating?

You paint his dick in Texans colors and he won't beat it for years

Why do the Cowboys want to change their name to the Dallas Tampons?

Because they are only good for one period and do not have a second string

What's the difference between
the Titans and the Taliban?

The Taliban has a running game

Where do you go in Tennessee
in case of a tornado?

LP Field, they never get a
touchdown there

Why do ducks fly over LP Field upside down?

There's nothing worth craping on

What do you call a Dallas Cowboy with a Super Bowl ring?

Senior Citizen

Terror Alert

The Titans football practice was delayed for nearly three hours yesterday after a player reported finding an unknown white powdery substance on the practice field.

Practice was stopped and the cops and the FBI were called in. After a complete analysis, FBI forensic experts determined that the white substance unknown to these players was in fact the goal line. Practice resumed after Special Agents decided the team was unlikely to encounter the substance again this season.

There's a rumor that after the current sponsorship expires the Colts have lined up a new sponsor, Tampax

They thought it was an appropriate change as the club is going through a very bad period

What's the difference between John Wayne Bobbitt and Jerry Jones?

Jones cut off his own Johnson

Why did Tony Romo cross the road?

To get to the hospital on the other side

Why are the Dallas Cowboys
like Hillary Clinton?

Both have Bills to push around

Matt Hasselbeck just threw his iPhone 5 in frustration but it was intercepted and returned for a touchdown

What Does the Dallas Cowboys and the movie Broke Back Mountain have in common?

They both have cowboys that suck

Why is Matt Hasselbeck unable to answer a telephone?

He can't find the receiver

Did you know the Cowboys had a 11 and 5 season this year?

11 arrests, 5 convictions

Why doesn't El Paso have a professional football team?

Because then Dallas would want one too

Tony Romo continues to impress, he managed to complete 5 passes to the Chicago Bears on Monday Night.

Someone should tell him he plays for the Dallas Cowboys.

After the game, Matt Hasselbeck threw his helmet towards the sideline in disgust and that too was intercepted

Printed in Great Britain
by Amazon.co.uk, Ltd.,
Marston Gate.